CONTENTS

The State of the Art Quilt:

Contemporary Quilts for the Collector

edited by **Barbara Packer**

THE STATE OF THE ART QUILT:
Contemporary Quilts for the Collector

Published in conjunction with Quilt Expo '85,
an exhibition shown at Sands Point Preserve, Sands Point, New York.

This publication has been made possible by a grant from the
Roslyn Savings Bank.

☰ROSLYN

Additional copies may be ordered from:

> Friends of Nassau County Recreation
> P.O. Box 456
> East Meadow, New York 11554

Photography: Stan Garfield Assoc., Inc./Mark Leslie

Color separations: East Coast Graphics

Typesetting and printing: William T. Swengros, Inc.

Book and Cover Design: Barbara Packer and Susan Langan

Cover: *(detail)* Esther Parkhurst. *July Study*

Preface

The objective of Quilt Expo is twofold: to present a pictorial survey of today's quilt scene for examination by the collector, and to direct serious attention to the study of the contemporary quilt as an art form. Other catalogs have handsomely displayed the quilts of many fine artists and, in so doing, have earned a larger audience for and a greater appreciation of the rich and vital creations of these artists. The present volume is intended to continue the admirable work of its predecessors but also to suggest another path: namely, the study of quilts in the context of art, not merely craft, history. Our aim has been to combine quality photographic reproductions of contemporary quilts with serious—to many minds, long overdue—writing about them.

The claim of quilts on the collector of contemporary art has both a pragmatic and an aesthetic dimension; it is a matter of both sense and sensibility. Very simply, buying contemporary quilts is a good investment. Although quiltmakers who work within such recognizably modern and post-modern categories as expressionism, Op, Pop, and Minimalist still receive fewer rewards, both monetary and critical, than their counterparts in painting and sculpture, this situation is slowly beginning to change. Critics and collectors are coming to see quiltmaking as a unique American phenomenon, as an art without European models; like the Abstract Expressionism of Jackson Pollock or the "romances" of Hawthorne and Melville, quiltmaking was born on native ground and out of an "original response" to native circumstances. What has been said of Le Corbusier could be applied to quilt artists: "Form [is] form. . . no matter whether it turn[s] up in painting, in sculpture or in building." Contemporary quilts offer the collector not only the formalized vision of art but also the texture of living things.

Barbara Packer
New York City
March 1985

INTRODUCTION

Perhaps no other American art form possesses greater appeal or familiarity than the quilt. Physically and emotionally, it has warmed Americans from every walk of life for generations. Its rich tradition has spanned the centuries and continued from the first days of our nation to the present.

Much has been written about the history of quiltmaking, and it is now well known. Primarily a woman's art, quiltmaking developed in response to the functional concerns of our ancestors. Colonial women fashioned quilts from two layers of fabric filled with wool or cotton held in place by stitched designs. To avoid wasting cloth, they often assembled their quilt tops from scraps. Practicality and function were prime concerns: these quilts provided warmth and comfort during the harsh winters while making frugal use of available materials. Although they were roughly made, these early quilts were the precursors of the pieced quilts which ultimately became established as one of America's most important design traditions.

That this tradition has continued, unbroken, is remarkable. The industrial advances of the nineteenth century produced machine-made coverlets which eroded the need to make quilts. Later, the advent of central heating helped to make quiltmaking functionally obsolete. And yet, concurrent with these developments, American women created some of the finest and most elaborate examples of the art. Most of their quilts were designed for use, but the impetus to make them was often a greater reflection of aesthetic impulse than of utilitarian need. Quiltmaking offered women the opportunity to explore color and design and to give visual expression to themes from the world around them.

Many quilts made today continue to mirror the hundreds of patterns handed down over time. However, the past fifteen years have also seen a new American quilt taking shape. This is due, in part, to the general growth of the craft movement and the appreciation of the handmade which it has fostered. In addition, antique quilts have undergone a reevalua-tion which has emphasized the excellence and invention of their design, and moved them from the bed to the wall where they are appreciated as art objects in their own right. This acknowledgment that a quilt can be a significant work of art has been critical to the development of the new quilt. The feminist movement has also played an important role. Through focusing on the quilt as a central element in women's artistic heritage, it has prompted numerous women artists to explore the quilt's potential as a vehicle of contemporary expression, thus allying themselves with a vital tradition.

The contemporary quilt differs from its historical predecessor in many ways. It is often created by an artist with formal fine-art training in a discipline such as painting, printmaking, sculpture, or architecture. Frequently, it is designed primarily or solely as a visual statement, with its traditional utilitarian function a secondary consideration, at most. Since the new quilt is likely to be divorced from the role of bed covering, it is no longer essential for it to retain a regular shape, and it is free to depart from the rectangle with curved or zigzagged edges, or even to take on sculptural dimension. Materials such as paper or plastic are sometimes used in the construction of this quilt, and its surface design incorporates images which reflect the modern world. Twentieth-century technology has also had an impact: today's quiltmaker often employs color xeroxing, blueprinting, photo-screen printing, or other nontraditional decorative techniques.

Frequently, the results of these pioneering efforts are works of art more closely related to the other visual arts than to traditional quilts. An interest in pattern, the restraint of minimalism, and the return of realism are some of the current trends which have found expression in quiltmaking. The best of the new quilts are strong artistic statements which combine arresting visual imagery with the tactile quality inherent in the fiber media.

Clearly, the quilt is in the process of evolution, with

some contemporary examples challenging even the fundamental issue of what makes a quilt a quilt. And with this definition in transition, the question of what the nature of quiltmaking is arises.

Traditionally, fabric and stitching have been essential to the quilt, and they are still intrinsic to contemporary works. It is the process of assembling layers of fabric and stitching them together that sets the quilt apart from the other fiber arts. Although the surface of the contemporary quilt may be embellished through techniques such as painting or printing, layers of stitched fabric are still its foundation.

As the contemporary quilt has developed, quilt like works created from such materials as paper or plastic have challnged this basic assumption. In image or technique, they make reference to the quilt's tradition. Like traditional pieced quilts, they are collages of various parts gathered together and assembled, and they are often layered and finally stitched.

These works raise important considerations for the collector of contemporary quilts. Unlike the collector of traditional or antique pieces, he must consider the very nature of the quilt to form his criteria for decision making. Originality of design and excellence of craftsmanship are other primary concerns.

One couple with a growing collection of contemporary quilts first collected antique quilts. They are now committed to contemporary pieces. Although they have collected only fabric quilts to date, they feel that it is an error to define the new quilt without room for flexibility. "It is important," they note, "to keep an open mind and not to rule out nontraditional works too quickly." Their personal emotional reaction to each work in their collection has determined how and what they collect. With the enthusiastic response characteristic of true collectors, they state simply that the love of quilts is their reason for collecting. They see the role of the collector as being significant in several respects. When the collector purchases the works of young or unknown artists, he provides them with the encouragement necessary to develop their work. In addition, through financial support, the collector allows the artist to pursue his work with freedom, lessening the need felt by some artists to produce pieces of commercial appeal. By sharing his collection through loans, the collector helps to provide greater exposure and increase the artist's audience. In this way, he helps to inform the public, to encourage ideas to multiply among artists, and even to inspire others to collect.

Today, there are few private collections of contemporary quilts. Corporations are beginning to collect them, quiltmakers themselves are assembling collections through trades, and many private collectors purchase a single piece as part of a larger art collection. Only a small number have made contemporary quilts their focus.

This may be due to several factors. The contemporary quilt itself is still somewhat new. There are relatively few artists creating it, and each of them may produce only three or four pieces per year. Therefore, the new quilt does not exist in great numbers. Lack of exposure is another reason cited by many artists and gallery owners for the scarcity of collecting. They feel that, to many collectors, the contemporary quilt is yet unknown.

Artists, dealers, and collectors alike agree that exhibitions will play a major role in overcoming these obstacles and fostering new collecting. To the collector with foresight, they will demonstrate the vitality and excitement of the contemporary quilt. And through his patronage, the pioneering collector will participate in shaping the future of a strong tradition in American art.

Kathleen Nugent Mangan
Curator
American Craft Museum
February, 1985

The Rise of the Contemporary Art Quilt

by Martin Karlow

About thirty-five years ago, an unprecedented event occurred in the art of Western painting: after centuries of representing real worlds or fashioning visionary ones, it began to aspire to the condition of the traditionally abstract and nonmimetic medium known as quiltmaking. Unfortunately nobody bothered to notice—at least from the presepctive of quiltmaking.

From the perspective of painting, however, it has been chronicled again and again. The New York art critic Leo Steinberg, for example, speaks of a shift in painters' conception of the picture plane from vertical to horizontal. Until "around 1950," he writes, "the conception of the picture as representing a world, some sort of worldspace which reads on the picture plane in correspondence with the erect human posture"[1] remained operative. "The top of the picture corresponds to where we hold our heads aloft; while its lower edge gravitates to where we place our feet. Even in Picasso's Cubist collages, where the Renaissance worldspace concept almost breaks down, there is still a harking back to implied acts of vision, to something that was once actually seen." In this sense, even the Abstract Expressionists are "still nature painters. Pollock's drip paintings cannot escape being read as thickets; Louis' *Veils* acknowledge the same gravitational force to which our being in nature is subject."[2]

But thirty-five years ago, a "radical shift" occurred, a shift from a vertical point-of-view to what Steinberg calls "the flatbed picture plane," a shift from "artists who use paint and surface to suggest existences other than surface and painting"[3] to artists like Robert Rauschenberg and Dubuffet whose pictures "no longer simulate vertical fields, but opaque flatbed horizontals"; such pictures "no more depend on head-to-toe correspondence with human posture than a newspaper does." They make their "symbolic allusion" to "surfaces such as tabletops, studio floors, charts, bulletin boards" . . . and beds.

Here are a few outrageous examples from Rauschenberg's early oeuvre. For an exhibition on the subject of "nature in art," the artist submitted a square patch of growing grass held down by chicken wire, placed in a box, and hung on a wall (he periodically visited the museum with a watering can); it is impossible to conceive of a more concrete example of the shift Steinberg describes than this. Similarly, in the famous *Drawing by Willem de Kooning Erased by Robert Rauschenberg* "he was making more than a multifaceted psychological gesture; he was changing—for the viewer no less than for himself—the angle of imaginative confrontation; tilting de Kooning's evocation of a worldspace into a thing produced by pressing down on a desk."[4] Most striking of all in the present context is his *Bed*(1955), a picture literally composed of a pillow and a real quilt *Bed* and Rauschenberg's other combine-paintings are no longer analogues of "a world perceived from an upright position," but are instead "matrix[es] of information conveniently placed in a vertical situation." Though meant to be hung on walls, they keep "referring back to the horizontals on which we walk and sit, work and sleep."

Now it happens that for many generations the horizontal on which we sleep was the exclusive domain and showcase for the art of quilting, and Steinberg's ingenious theory takes on a new and lustrous relevance when we think in quilterly terms—especially when we recall that "around 1950" people lacked the temerity either to hang quilts from walls or to call themselves artists when they created them for real, horizontal beds. Thirty-five years later we see quilts on walls without blinking an eye. Even more, quilts that function exclusively as vertical art works are continually made and sold and hung, and at this point in time to consider actually sleeping on or under such quilts makes about as much sense as actually shooting arrows at a Jasper Johns target.

Steinberg, without intending to, makes us realize that this change in the status of the quilt, a shift of considerable magnitude in the history of this medium, did not happen overnight. Although we all witnessed it and although quilters benefited enor-

Martin Karlow is a freelance writer and quilt collector.

mously from it, this change has gone unchronicled in the annals of quiltmaking. When it is examined from Steinberg's art-historical perspective, however, we get a glimpse of how gratuitous and ironic a change it was. Gratuitous because quilters were the indirect beneficiaries of other artists' struggles and breakthroughs, artists in other media, and ironic because this "most radical shift" in the art world amounts in effect to no more in the quilt world than a belated recognition of, and catching up with, what quilters had been practicing for roughly two hundred years. Quilters, it could be said, were the real pioneers of the flatbed picture plane insofar as their "special mode of imaginative confrontation," the "psychic address" of their images (to use Steinberg's terms), had never been anything but horizontal all along. Thus, by a mere act of physical placement—off the bed and onto the wall—the quilter can perhaps belatedly get her just historical deserts: she becomes, as it were instantly, a precursor of the avant-garde.

Without intending to, Steinberg makes artists like Rauschenberg appear in retrospect to have been involved in an unwitting conspiracy to exalt the essential and inherent qualities of the quilt medium. He shows us one way of coming to grips with this extraordinary change in all its gratuitousness and irony and suggests a larger context in which we can at last begin to understand its inevitably exhilarating effects on quilters. In the following pages, I would like to suggest a few others in the belief that this effort is long overdue.

Unwitting conspiracy may sound like too strong a term, but a brief look at some influential essays by two of the better-known critics of the sixties, Susan Sontag and Clement Greenberg, should prove otherwise.

In the title essay of *Against Interpretation*(1966), Sontag described the parameters of a sensibility, which, though neither new nor uniquely American, was a hitherto unarticulated part of many young people's—and here I include young quiltmakers and young artists who for no *apparent* reason would soon become quiltmakers—cultural identity. The interpretation Sontag was against is the kind associated with devotees of Freud and Marx but practiced by humanists in general. These interpreters look *behind* or *beyond* the work for meaning, which they tend to summarize in social, political, or moral terms; they value any specific work insofar as it proves itself to be a profound "criticism of life," as Matthew Arnold put it. What makes a given work great, according to this view, is its content. What the work *says,* not what it *does,* is its essence. This amounts, Sontag writes, "to

the philistine refusal to leave the work of art alone. Real art has the capacity to make us nervous. By reducing the work to its content and then interpreting *that,* one tames the work of art. Interpretation makes art manageable, conformable."[5]

Anyone who ever suffered through a college literature course—heard a professor dig "behind" a text to find a latent but "truer" subtext (which the student himself missed in his own reading and so dutifully copies down in his notebook and then spews back on an exam), heard symbols explicated and themes paraphrased and, when term-paper time rolled around, turned desperately to articles *about* the work rather than the work itself and his own responses while reading it—knows that Sontag is giving voice to his own experience, that "Against Interpretation" is not part of an ongoing argument among highbrows but a statement about his own sad, baffling, ultimately tedious encounters with art in college.

In place of an aesthetic of illusory depth, of an ever-receding, metaphysical heart of darkness the critic penetrates and captures, Sontag offers an aesthetic of the surface. "Man is a creature who is designed to live on the surface; he lives in the depths—whether terrestrial, oceanic, or psychological—at his peril," she writes in an essay on the novelist Nathalie Sarraute.[6] If criticism is not an attempt to usurp a work but to serve it, it must pay more attention to matters of style and form or attempt to "supply a really accurate, sharp, loving description of the appearance of a work of art."[7]

Note the precise words: *accurate, sharp, and loving attention to the appearance of a work of art.* Sontag may be offering a richer, more erotic program for the critic, but her words, with their emphasis on the sheer materiality of art, describe the oldest impulse of the quiltmaker. What an ideal criticism should do turns out to be what quiltmakers always did do. "Ideally," Sontag writes, "it is possible to elude the interpreters. . . by making works of art whose surface is so unified and clean, whose momentum is so rapid, whose address is so direct that the work can be. . .just what it is."[8] Such immediacy, of course, characterizes much of the most interesting art of the sixties and seventies, but it requires only the smallest leap of the imagination to see that the quilt, in its own, non-mainstream, "craft"-rather-than-"art" way, had realized this condition since its inception. But of course neither Sontag nor anyone else was thinking in terms of quiltmaking.

Certainly Clement Greenberg, in a much-discussed and much-maligned essay called "Modernist Painting" (1965), wasn't, yet he, even more than Sontag, unintentionally formulated a contemporary aesthetic that brought many recent manifestations of the avant-garde close to the oldest practices of quilt-makers.[9] Like Sontag, Greenberg argues against interpretation—i.e., against "literary" content in painting, against illusionistic space and subject matter—but he does not believe contemporary artists to be in flight from or deliberately reacting against habitual notions. Rather than striving, to be audaciously original, artists have been striving, in Greenberg's view, to state more explicitly those properties that belong uniquely to their medium. The history of any given medium thereby becomes an ongoing effort of purification, of eliminating all elements not exclusive to its domain.

Like all systematic reductions, Greenberg's theory of modernism makes major artists that fail to fit its formulas appear to be minor artists (his assessment of Jasper Johns is a notorious example). But like the best of reductive theorists, he also dispels many of the ostensible difficulties in newer art, allowing us to take pleasure, for example, in the performance of a Merce Cunningham work that might otherwise provoke the hulking philistine in us to righteous wrath. Instead of seeing Cunningham's choreography as a direct attack upon our preconceptions of what dance is supposed to be, we can see that the artist is ridding his medium of extradance elements: of psychology, story, even music. Greenberg's ideas help us not to see Cunningham as an avatar of modern art's recurrent Dada syndrome, which he is not, and allows us to see him as the didactic explorer he truly is.[10]

In the case of painting, the individual limitations are flatness, the shape of the support, and the properties of pigment. Taking these limitations as his starting point, Greenberg argues that contemporary painting does not so much break with the past as it reverses traditional practices in the name of a purer, more independent art. The opposition between surface and depth, for example, has always existed; whereas the Old Masters invited us to witness what was inside the flatness of a painting before we became aware of the flatness itself, the contemporary painter, reversing the distinction, makes us aware of the painting as painting first, and what the flatness contains second. In doing this, he is motivated neither by aggression toward the traditions of high art nor by the desire to épater le bourgeoisie; he is not attempting to "subvert" his discipline "but to entrench it more firmly in its area of competence."[11] In this sense, Western art has always

been inherently abstract, but its abstractness was deceptive, accessory, negative; the modernist reversal of priorities renders abstract form overt, primary, positive. The modernist rejects the illusion of three-dimensionality because the third dimension does not properly belong to painting's peculiar province; it belongs to the unique and peculiar competencies and limitations of sculpture, and so, for its own autonomy, painting has had to banish it. Two-dimensionality—flatness and flatness alone—belongs exclusively to painting; therefore painting has oriented itself to flatness with a vengeance.

What, we may ask, does this mean in terms of quiltmaking? For one thing, Greenberg's deemphasis of the role of modeling and value contrasts and his emphasis on the optical sensation of color brings painting closer to quiltmaking than any of us, I would imagine, ever considered possible. Yet there is nothing forced about the connection: the property of opticality belongs to quiltmaking as undeniably as it belongs to painting; it differentiates both media from sculpture but neither from the other.

For another thing, two-dimensionality is, and always has been, a given for the quiltmaker; the three-dimensional quilt is the exception not the rule. Finally, extravisual meaning—content, whether literary or symbolic—has never been in the quiltmaker's area of competence; it may be a goal an individual quiltmaker strives for, but in doing so, she is subverting (in Greenberg's terms) the properties that belong exclusively to her medium as well as the painter's

It is perhaps ironic that painting should have had to purge itself of a long history of extraneous forms and unnatural effects in order to arrive at precisely the point where quiltmaking began, and it is certainly a consequence of this theory Greenberg did not consider, but ironic or not, the coincidence is there, and once we recognize it, outdated notions about the quilt's status as art must crumble. This remains true whether we find Greenberg's ideas valid or, as his detractors have called them, "preventive." It remains true because as the "voice" of Post-Painterly Abstraction, Greenberg articulated the ambitions and called attention to the achievements of the painters now known as color-field abstractionists and minimalists, painters whose flat, optical, "meaningless" images don't *say* much to us but *do* to us what quilts have always done to us—simply by being quilts. As a medium that had never been encumbered with illusionist space and subject matter or obliged to mean something beyond or behind what it was in any given work, quiltmaking had always been what painting in the 1960s came to be.

Seeing the connection was merely a matter of physical placement: off the bed and onto the wall.

It could conceivably be argued that many earlier paintings, those of Mondrian for example, were flat and geometric and abstract yet they failed to precipitate a renaissance in quiltmaking or effect any change in the status of the quilt as art object, and therefore the correlation I find between events in the art world and their reverberations on quiltmaking is not valid. But Mondrian's paintings are flat only in relation to what came before them; his canvases are still illusionistic in a way the color-field abstractionists and minimalist paintings of the sixties are not. A Mondrian still contains, that is to say, a theater of forms; the spectator's eye is still invited to penetrate the interior, whereas a painting by Frank Stella or Kenneth Noland, like so many quilts both old and new, invites the eye to skid laterally across the surface but not to enter.

The inherent flatness of quilts makes them ancestors of Noland's or Stella's work, ancestors too of the flatness of color-field abstractionists like Helen Frankenthaler or Morris Louis. In the latters' work, paint is stained directly onto raw canvas; it soaks directly into, rather than becoming a layer on top of, the surface. By these means, Frankenthaler and Louis achieve the maximum opticality in their work, which is their goal, but they also, incidentally, achieve a quilterly effect: the painter's surface becomes, literally, a piece of white cloth subjected to dyeing—it becomes, in short, fabric. Unless the quiltmaker breaks with her tradition and reverses Morris and Frankenthaler by painting on top of her material, color in her work, as in theirs, is not layered onto but is coextensive with surface.

By the same token, it could be argued that when a quilt looks, say, like a Stella, the parallel is provocative but deceptive, even spurious. Stella's work "means" something, the argument would run, while the quiltmaker's aim is "merely" decorative; granted that by refusing to *draw* with paint, Stella accidentally (in his protractor series, for exampl) *strip-pieces* with paint, constructing in geometric blocks of color, the fact still remains that his intention, as a creator of high art, was different from the lowly quiltmaker's. As a reply to this argument, Stella's own words are sufficient:

I always get into arguments with people who want to retain the old values in painting—the humanistic values that they always find on the canvas. If you pin them down, they always end up asserting that there is something there besides the paint on the canvas. My painting is based on the fact that only what can be seen there *is* there. It really is an object. . . If the painting were lean enough, accurate enough or right enough, you would just be able to look at it. All I want anyone to get out of my paintings, and all I ever get out of them, is the fact that you can see the whole idea without any confusion. . . . What you see is what you see.[12].

For Frank Stella, there is no point where the (merely) decorative stops and the meaningfully pictorial begins. His work, like the best work of quiltmakers, surmounts the distinction between the decorative and the dramatic, subsumes both in a design whose only justification is itself.

The flight from interpretation and its corollary, the attack upon what many artists felt to be an impoverished tradition of meaningful content, contributed much toward priming us for a rediscovery of the artistry of quiltmaking. Critics like Sontag and Greenberg tell us volumes about the tacit assumptions of generations of quiltmakers, and the fact that neither critic ever mentions quilts only makes them more fun to read from a quiltmaking prespective—which may sound like a rationalization for the absence of serious critical works on the subject but is truly not meant to be. Nevertheless, ideas filter down slowly or not at all unless they are expressed in concrete works of art which, even if they are not understood, are seen and, through the endless reproductions of our mechanical age, seen again. It is for this reason that quiltmakers owe a debt for their newfound status to artists like Frank Stella, Helen Frankenthaler, Morris Lewis, and Vasarely. As one quiltmaker I know put it: "Like the citizens of a geographically remote and politically insignificant colony annexed to a great empire-building nation in its heyday of military expansion and economic prosperity, quiltmakers have flourished at a remove from the centers of activity, and have shared substantially, if indirectly, in the spoils of spiritual and aesthetic wars won by another nation's generals and another nation's soldiers."

A debt is also owed to the artists who helped break down the once-rigid distinctions between high art and low art, and to the artists who helped blur, often beyond recognition, received ideas about what kinds of materials were proper for crafts and what was proper for art. A work like Sam Gilliam's *Carousel Form II* (1969), a soaked and splattered canvas that was left permanently unstretched, breaks down the distinction between painting and sculpture; by staining his canvas with acrylic in the manner of the color-field abstractionists, Gilliam asserts its status as a painting; by draping it like a curtain, he suggests at the same time that it is sculpture and fabric art. Similarly, the *Planks*(1967) of the West Coast artist John Mc-

Cracken, oblongs of wood or fiberglass that were sprayed with automobile lacquer and then stood on the floor or leaned against the wall of a gallery, defy classification as either painting or sculpture; they collapse the two media into a third, as-yet-unnamed convention (to many people, they looked like little more than M&M-colored two-by-fours). Such ambiguous art works loosen prejudices about crafts as opposed to arts and are the antecedents of those quilts whose makers use airbrushing, photo-silkscreening, color xeroxing, even colored paper instead of fabric, without ceasing to be quiltmakers.

The debt is also owed to artists who reacted against cult of the person and against the tragic-heroic note so often struck by the Abstract Expressionists. "It was a journey that one must make, walking straight and alone," wrote Clyfford Still in a letter reprinted in the catalog of a 1959 show, "until one had crossed the darkened and wasted valleys and come out at last into the clear air and could stand on the high and limitless plain. Imagination, no longer fettered by the laws of fear, became as one with vision. And the Act, intrinsic and absolute, was its meaning, and the bearer of its passion."[13] A quilter's patient fingers might well stiffen in such rarified late-Transcendentalist air, causing her to reply, along with Marcel Duchamp, that "Art has absolutely no existence as veracity, as truth. People always speak of it with this great, religious reverence, but why should it be so revered... No, I'm afraid I'm an agnostic in art. I don't believe in it with all the mystical trimmings. As a drug it's very useful for a number of people, very sedative, but as a religion it's not even as good as God."[14] Quiltmakers are more apt to feel, along with Frank Stella, "very strongly about finding a way that wasn't so wrapped up in the hullabaloo...something that was stable in a sense, something that wasn't constantly a record of your own sensitivity."[15] Duchamp and Stella found this way, a cooler, less Dionysiac and self-enraptured way, and quiltmakers, who tend to share such a sensibility, owe them more than thanks.

Quiltmakers even owe thanks to Abstract Expressionists like Still, Pollock, and Barnett Newman — occasional sententiousness notwithstanding — the sheer size of whose paintings has probably done more than anything I have hitherto mentioned to prepare our eyes and minds for the untroubled acceptance of a quilt on a wall. We have become inured to enormity and tend to forget that only since 1949, when Pollock and Newman created their first big canvases, has the large canvas become the rule, not the exception. Just as the radical departures of Frank Stella coincided visually with some of the oldest quilting practices — a paradox previously noted — so the Abstract Expressionists' earlier revolution in scale resulted in canvases whose outrageous lengths and widths were often identical to the specifications to which quilts had, ironically, always conformed.

The coincidence extends further, for the wall-size paintings of the Abstract Expressionists contain no scale referent to the world of external objects; this was a first in the history of anti-illusionism, and therefore a first in the history of Western painting, yet again, it was something quiltmakers had been doing all along. The only difference lies in the fact that no one thought to hang a quilt on a wall, and this is precisely the point: had it not been for Pollock and Newman and Still, it is possible that no one ever would have. Once the big canvas had established its hegemony, it remained for the painters of Frank Stella's generation to adopt a "cooler," less personal and Romantic form of address, and suddenly, strangely quiltlike objects began appearing on gallery and later museum walls. All the quiltmaker needed to do was sit up and notice — and perhaps gasp.

Call it luck or call it a conspiracy unwittingly plotted and carried out by the denizens of the "higher" arts. Whatever we call it, the result is the same: the quiltmaker's art had come of age.

It was simply a matter of physical placement: off the bed and onto the wall.

NOTES

1. Leo Steinberg, *Other Criteria: Confrontations with Twentieth-Century Art.* New York: Oxford University Press, 1972; p. 82.

2. *Ibid.,* p. 84.

3. *Ibid.,* p. 42.

4. *Ibid.,* pp. 86–87.

5. Susan Sontag, *Against Interpretation.* New York: Dell Publishing Co., 1969; p. 17.

6. *Ibid.,* p. 115.

7. *Ibid..,* p. 22.

8. *Ibid.,* p. 21.

9. "Modernist Painting" first appeared in Art and Literature (No. 4, Spring 1965). The version referred to above is contained in Gregory Battcock ed., *The New Art: A Critical Anthology.* New York: E. P. Dutton & Co., 1966; pp. 100–111.

10. According to Barbara Rose the European movement known as Dada (the word was first used in 1916) was "anti-art, antiwar, antimaterialism, and antirationalism"; its repudiation and satirizing of bourgeois values "suited the disenchanted mood of American intellectuals as the country was on the verge of World War I" (*American Art since 1900.* New York: Holt, Reinhart & Winston, 1975; p. 77). Ever since, the term "Dada" has come in handy as a way of labeling (and thereby coping with) the first appearance of anything new in art. For example, when Jasper Johns' now-famous flags and targets began showing up in galleries in the late fifties, *Newsweek* (March 31, 1958) reported that "Dada, it seems, rides again," and *Time* (May 4, 1959), in a piece entitled "His Heart Belongs to Dada," informed us that "like Johns, the Dadaists deliberately tried to strip art of all sentiment and all significance." Now that the critical appreciation of Johns' work has caught up with its subject, the label seems absurd.

11. Greenberg *op. cit.,* p. 101.

12. Bruce Glaser, "Questions to Stella and Judd," *Art News* (September 1966); reprinted in Ellen H. Johnson, ed., *American Artists on Art: From 1940 to 1980.* New York: Harper & Row, 1982; p. 117.

13. Quoted in Calvin Tomkins, *Off the Wall: The Art World of Our Time.* Garden City, N.Y.: Doubleday & Co., 1980; p. 124.

14. *Ibid.,* p. 128.

15. *Ibid.,* p. 168.

Why Do Artists Quilt?

by Jan Myers

The question "Why do quilters quilt?" has several easy answers: we love the feel of the material in our hands; we like the act of sewing, of constructing greater wholes out of a series of parts; we love the product, the warm, portable sensuousness of quilts; we find it satisfying to be part of a continuous tradition that is rooted to some degree in our personal and national histories.

Do these same answers apply to the question "Why do *artists* quilt?" All of them do, to a greater or lesser degree for each artist who is asked. More at issue is the following question: "If you really consider yourself to be an artist, why work in a medium that is not traditionally accepted, and may never be accepted, as an art medium by the art establishment?" Pan Studstill states the reality quite simply: "I relate better to the art community than they do to me." Nancy Erickson expressed the same difficulty: "There is a tendency, perhaps justified, to say, 'Why don't you do that in drawing?' Or, perhaps, 'What are your paintings like?' People in the so-called fine arts see a division between a fabric quilt and a painting or a sculpture, but this will change, just as our work will change. But it's well to confuse this whole issue—I enter painting shows whenever possible." This is how Terrie Hancock Mangat expressed the problem:

I have a friend who is the head of a large university art department. He told me that he likes everything about my quilts except that they are quilts. No matter how good they get artistically, to him they will never be art because they are quilts. A lot of quilters think that my quilts have too much junk and weirdness to be quilts. They like my old work better. Maybe I'll work myself out of an audience. But it doesn't matter. Most non-art-educated people who look at my quilts feel something strongly about them, even the abstract ones. The fabric helps everyday people relate to the piece. Maybe quilts are the "working man's art." I feel like my quilts are on the outer edge of being quilts (some of them) and some are on the outer edge of being art. They are straddling the line like a lot of other things in my life.

In these words, Mangat captures the essential dilemma of the quiltmaker. On the one hand, quilters work in a medium that has traditionally been considered decorative, functional, and therapeutic, and which must, by all means, aim to be beautiful. On the other, Mangat realizes that if artists who are working in the quilt medium attempt to extend their creative vision, they may go beyond the boundaries of "quiltness" accepted by other quilters. Nancy Halpern suggests how preconceptions about quilts stifle the quiltmaker/artist: "Fabrics are soft. Bedding is soft. Quiltmakers tend to deal in soft ideas, in gentleness, in the soothing and therapeutic nature of both sleep and bedding. When they don't, when the try to say something tough. . . in this medium, their work can be aggressive or just plain disturbing. . . . They cut off a large part of their constituency, the Sleepers and Dreamers who want to wrap themselves up (visually, if not literally) in beautiful, portable shelters."

Is it only in challenging the "comfort" of quilts that quiltmakers gain status as artists? Is there some sort of inverse ratio between accessibility and art? Does the fact that the man on the street can respond passionately to a quilt somehow disqualify the quilt as a piece of "high" art?

And so, the "art vs. craft" debate rages on, and probably it always will. Personally, I find it tedious and on the whole irrelevant. When I am asked, "Do you consider yourself an artist or do you consider yourself a craftsperson?" I have only one answer: "Yes." It is not an either/or question for me. It is quite a simple matter to declare myself an artist, but we all know it doesn't make me one. My work must speak for itself, and that is clear; my aesthetic pronouncements have no bearing on its quality. Speaking of her anomalous position as both a quilter and an artist, Debra Millard observes:

The support and approval I get from other quilters often provides me with creative energy and a reason to continue. . . . I feel less comfortable about my place in the art community. I often do not feel acceptance as a equal, and am left with the impression that I am working in an "inferior" medium. This used to bother me a lot and I used to fight to explain my position to other artists working in more traditional media. I have recently decided that what I was really doing was trying to convince myself that I was really an artist. Once I reached the point of knowing that I am working as an artist, the explanation of my position has become increasingly less important. It still bothers me that some will not even consider the possibility of my work as art, but basically I have decided that it is their ignorance and not a problem in my creative work.

Almost without exception, the artists who were asked the question "Why quilts?" affirmed the nature and creative potential of the materials. Any sentimental, political, or feminist motivations were secondary. "I don't feel I ever really understood how to paint, because I never really related to the materials. From the first, I felt a good relationship to quilt materials. . . the *feel* of the materials. . . the constructive process itself" (Michael James). "I turned to

Jan Myers is a quilt artist whose work is represented in many private and corporate collections.

fabric because I wanted to see what the effect of different levels of texture had on the color interaction. . . the pattern in fabric seduced me further away from my formula approach" (Nancy Hermann). "A new medium, new textures, a whole new way of looking at form, and color—all these were what fabric brought. One can try this color and that, and see what works best. There's the wonder of the kaleidoscope ever present. Plus textures. Plus being able to draw and paint on fabric too. Plus being able to roll all this up in a box and send it off UPS. . . all over the world" (Nancy Erickson). "Quiltmaking processes satisfy my artistic needs best of any media I have tried. I work from an emotional core. In quiltmaking, my creative process is more direct and more intuitive" (Nancy Crow). "I have always loved fabrics; I love to manipulate them. The limitations of construction seem to provide me with the necessary stimulation and challenge. My love of color and of combining or merging certain patterned fabrics, which fractures colors, provide me with the means to develop my abstract work. The quilt medium seems to be perfect for me" (Esther Parkhurst).

These specific reactions to fabric—in short *how* we manipulate our materials—are as diverse as our work. Yet nearly all quilters find themselves working with "instant premixed color," as Terrie Mangat describes the prints and solids that inhabit her studio. Even those who are creating or altering their own fabrics (and the number is increasing as more quilters want to exert control over their raw materials), even those quilters who are actually *painting* on their fabric, are, in the end, using paint quite differently, in terms of both process and product, than painters. Pam Studstill remarks that quiltmaking is more challenging in a technical sense than her painting had been, "as one can't just mix up the colors and start working." This "collage aspect" of quiltmaking is the main attraction for Nancy Halpern: "Found fabrics, found relationships between fabrics, the gift of discovering unexpected correlations. . . of finding what I need, in some strange corner." So it would seem that for many quilters, what the medium may lack in spontaneity or directness of execution is made up for in the challenge and joy of dealing with the variety of available raw materials.

Inevitably, speed of execution, or lack of same, is an issue for most artists who are quilting. "The biggest challenge is dealing with the tedious hours spent putting the quilt together," notes Nancy Crow. Nancy Hermann goes so far as to say that she hates sewing.

Nancy Halpern asserts that she is "one of the slowest of all quiltmakers, and proud of it too. However, I intend to work harder on getting the *illusion* of spontaneity and fluidity into my quilts, even if in actuality it takes me forever." Pam Studstill compares her work in quilts with her other two-dimensional work: "The quilts are riskier in terms of time, materials, and emotional involvement. When I work on a new quilt for two or three weeks and then realize something is not right about it, it is a major frustration. A 'bad' or 'not right' painting can be crumpled and put out with the garbage, a minor disappointment."

However much of a drawback the deliberate pace of quiltmaking can at times seem, is clearly outweighed by the creative potential of the process. It all boils down to this: when we talk about fabrics, we talk in terms of "good relationships," "seduction," "stimulation." Virginia Jacobs affirms that she is quilting because it is "colorful, vivacious, personal, flexible, strong, soft. . . and the field has hardly begun to be explored." This seems to be the best news yet: that the creative potential of the medium is looked upon as ever-expanding. When asked the question "Do you think that good quilts will stand the test of time as art?" quilters unanimously answered "Yes." Michael James elaborated: "Without question. I also think that this most recent period of development—the last ten years when the 'studio quilt' developed as a new manifestation of the quiltmaking tradition—will be viewed as *the* pivotal stage in the metamorphosis of the quilt."

In writing this article, I did not want to prove that quilts are art, much less to provide criteria for determining the quality of any particular quilt. Indeed, I believe that it is the product, the individual quilt as much as the individual painting, not the materials out of which either was constructed, that must be judged as art or "not-art." It seems pompous and petty to predicate the value of any art object on the basis of the tools and materials used to create it. I wanted only to share some of the thoughts artists shared with me as they mused over the question "Why quilts?" What coalesces and lingers in my mind as I read over their answers is their regard for the fabric of it all, their awareness of the layers of possibilities open to the quiltmaker/artist, and their pleasure in mining the creative flexibility of quilting. After two centuries, the possibilities of quilting seem far from exhausted. If anything, we are just beginning to explore them.

Contemporary Quilts in the Corporate Environment

by Sandra Sider

What does a hotel in Knoxville have in common with a hospital in Missoula, a bank in New York, and two international manufacturers of tobacco products? These businesses are among the dozens of American corporations that have purchased contemporary quilts.

Although several corporations have featured antique quilts in their collections—notably Chase Manhattan Bank, IBM, Liberty Corporation, and Xerox—the purchasing of contemporary quilts is a relatively recent development. This trend in corporate collecting began just five or six years ago and is expanding rapidly. The majority of contemporary quilts now in corporate collections have been purchased since 1983. As of autumn of 1984, the quilts of more than forty American fiber artists are owned by American businesses.

Philip Morris Inc., whose sponsorship of various art events clearly places this corporation in the cultural limelight, leads corporate America in the acquisition of contemporary quilts. In 1983 alone, approximately 20 percent of their acquisition budget was spent on quilts, largely because Philip Morris—in what surely will be seen in years to come as a brilliant coup in the world of fiber art—purchased the entire collection entitled "The Artist and the Quilt." Currently on tour, this controversial group of contemporary quilts will return to Philip Morris at the end of this year and become part of the permanent art collection.

National juried contemporary quilt exhibitions, such as Quilt Expo '85, have definitely contributed to the rising popularity of this type of art work. It is no accident that the first corporate enthusiasm for contemporary quilts surfaced in 1980 following the overwhelming public response to Quilt National '79. "The New American Quilt" was mounted in the Spring of 1976 at the Museum of Contemporary Crafts (American Craft Museum) in New York. This groundbreaking museum exhibit first attuned the public to the exciting possibilities explored more fully in the biennial Quilt Nationals '79, '81, and 83. Artists in that show have now acquired international reputations as contemporary quiltmakers, with several of their pieces included in corporate collections.

At the same time that art consultants and interior designers were becoming more informed about the artistry of contemporary quilts, several thought-provoking articles discussing the purpose of art in corporate collections appeared in business and design magazines. The most pervasive point reiterated by the authors was that businesses should consider their art purchases as more than mere financial investments.

Many businesses are discovering that contemporary quilts fulfill the multidimensional requirements of successful corporate art. Contemporary quilts by established artists are a sound investment, with the purchase price reasonably based on the artist's popularity and visibility—from quilts beginning at $2000 and slightly less that can be purchased through art consultants to the $7000 and up commanded by an Ed Larson piece. Contemporary quilts provide an important decorative element in the public and private spaces where they are displayed, and their acoustical properties dampen excessive noise.

Judy Jedlicka, president of the Business Committee for the Arts, suggests that decorative needs can precede investment interests where corporate art is concerned. Some corporate collections evolve only after pieces are purchased for their decorative quality—for example, to enhance the walls and lobbies of a new corporate building. After living with the art for a while, corporate executives often decide to begin collecting in a serious manner.

Because of their visually active surfaces, contemporary quilts are literally changing the ways that business looks at art. Philip Esocoff, an architect in Washington, D.C., focuses on integrating art into architecture. For the recent renovation of a bank, Esocoff recommended installing a long quilted panel on the wall behind the tellers. Virginia Jacobs executed the piece, whose primary function was to provide acoustical relief from reflected sound inside the

Sandra Sider is a quiltmaker and freelance writer in New York.

tellers' area, which is enclosed by bulletproof glass. The vertical steel strips supporting the glass bothered Esocoff and his client; they wanted the art work to act as a visible "magnet," pulling customers toward it without interference from the steel strips. They discussed the problem with the glass company, which developed and now offers transparent silicon joints as a standard option for businesses with art work behind glass panels.

Where do businesses usually display contemporary quilts? The majority are mounted in public spaces, such as plazas and lobbies, with dining areas singled out as especially appropriate display areas. Texaco's headquarters building in White Plains, New York, has a typical distribution of contemporary quilts: two in corporate dining rooms, one in a public space, and one in a private office.

Atlantic Ritchfield in Los Angeles reports "good reaction" to their quilts in private areas; Chase Manhattan praises the "very enthusiastic" response to their contemporary quilts in both private and public spaces. One particular international corporation with headquarters in the Southeast has found that the single contemporary quilt in their huge collection is the most popular piece they own.

An interesting reaction to contemporary quilts exhibited in corporate collections is from foreign visitors, some of whom are unfamiliar with quilts as a form of contemporary art. Foreigners remark upon the technical expertise and originality of design in these pieces and are most intrigued by contemporary quilts as unique expressions of indigenous American art. In the next few years foreign corporations will probably seek to acquire contemporary quilts. More foreign enthusiasm for contemporary quilts should be generated by the exhibit currently touring Japan, "Contemporary Quilts in Japan," and by another exhibit currently traveling to museums in France, "Quilts Contemporains Americains." Both these shows include invitational pieces by Nancy Crow and other noted fiber artists.

Corporate enthusiasm for contemporary quilts has already blossomed in the U.S. Several corporations without quilts of any type in their collections plan to acquire contemporary quilts in the future. Other corporations, who already own antique quilts, have expressed interest in adding contemporary quilts to their collections.

As for those businesess that have not yet considered contemporary quilts, Joanne Rapp of The Hand & The Spirit Crafts Gallery feels that this is simply because of lack of exposure. Her opinion is that perhaps the gallery world is in need of more traveling quilt shows such as Quilt Expo '85.

Contemporary quilts, a uniquely American art form that functions as decoration, investment, and a tribute to the technical excellence of generations of quiltmakers, will continue to appeal to corporate collectors. The annual shows of fine contemporary quilts that Quilt Expo promises to present should become touchstones of artistic quality.

Buff Hungerland. *Strings Attached: A Vinyl Quilt.*
1984. 42" x 36" x 2"
Mercer Island, Washington
Vinyl, cotton, polyester ribbon.
Fused vinyl pockets, stuffed with cotton broadcloth strips, joined with polyester ribbon.

All of this artist's work concerns transparency and opacity, color and value, and material contradictions. She tries to push materials beyond their usual use to create an image of simplicity and richness, one that is valuable through several layers of perception.

Mineko Kato. *Outer Limit.*
1984. 58" x 58"
Closter, N.J.
Cotton, blends. Machine-pieced and hand-quilted.

This is an original design based on the hexagon shape. The borders are diagonal strip piecing which enforces the direction toward the outer edges. Some fabrics were dyed with Japanese ink to create the proper shading and depth. Circular quilting also added further dimension.

Danae Anderson. *Floating World.*
1984. 48" x 45"
Ben Lomond, California
Hand-dyed, hand-silkscreened. Silk jacquards and brocades. Metallic fabrics and threads. Seminole patchwork and applique. Machine-pieced, hand-quilted.

This quilt is made up of silk jacquards which were hand-dyed or silkscreened by the artist. The "floating" triangles of color are interwoven with diagonal strips of red silk. The artist is interested in a composition which indicates change and movement and which implies spatial inconsistencies.

AWARD FOR INNOVATIVE USE OF MATERIALS

Clare M. Murray. *Soft Origami.*
1984. 41" x 38"
Canton, Ohio
Cottons. Hand-dyed and hand-painted, stamped, cut-throughs,
hand-appliqued machine-pieced, hand-quilted.

This combines one of the artist's favorite techniques, cutting through areas with narrow strips of fabric, and hand-dyeing and hand painting fabric. The combination of these techniques allowed the freedom needed to "float" the "fabric folds" on a background that was determined not by the color and print choices in the fabric store.

Clare M. Murray. *Daydreams.*
1983. 60" x 60"
Canton, Ohio
Cottons, blends. Strip-pieced, cut-throughs, hand-appliqued, machine-pieced, hand-quilted.

This is the first in a series consisting of the same four basic elements. The large strip-pieced sections and the triangle areas represent order, structure, and the artist's attitude toward her work and life. The two large windows represent the element of escape, often accomplished through dreaming, and finally the cut-through areas are meant to reflect a freer, less structured dream-like atmosphere.

Helen W. Richards. *At Autumn's End, All My Chrysanthemums Have Faded.*
1982. 44" x 43"
Tustin, California
Wool, felt, cotton velveteen, rayon challis. Appliqued and quilted.

While the artist has kept journals and written poetry, the form of prose-poetry that reached to her inner being was haiku, and she has constructed many images from these inspirations. Some are haikus she has written, others those that she admired. These lines created a sense of peace to know that even though the flowers fade, there is always another season, always another opportunity to self-express, there are no dead ends in eternity.

Judy B. Dales. *Octagon Mosaic.*
1984. 78" x 78"
Boonton Township, New Jersey
Cottons, blends, rayon challis. Hand-pieced, hand-quilted.

Octagon Mosaic is one of a series of quilts inspired by Islamic geometric art. This design is based on a repetitive circular grid in which each circle is divided into eight segments. The entire quilt is hand-pieced and the narrow strips between the star motifs were added to accentuate the tile mosaic effect. Eighty-six different prints were used to produce the rich tone of this intricate design.

INVITATIONAL

Esther Parkhurst. *March Study.*
1984. 56" x 53"
Los Angeles, California
Cottons, blends. Machine-strip-pieced. Hand-quilted.

BEST IN SHOW

Esther Parkhurst. *February Study.*
1984. 48" x 45"
Los Angeles, California
Cottons. Machine-strip-pieced, Hand-quilted.

The artist works intuitively with a trial and error method. She is dealing with movement, the translucent quality of light and shadow, but most of all the properties of color, which is a never ending discovery and challenge process.

BEST IN SHOW

Danae Anderson. *Antarctica Series: Icefalls.*
1984. 74" x 58"
Ben Lomond, California
Silk brocades and jacquards and silk gauze. Metallic fabric and thread.
Seminole patchwork, applique. Machine-pieced and hand-quilted.

This work is composed of minutely pieced silk jacquards and brocades which are separated by "rivers" of silk gauze. Diagonal strips of silk and floating triangular shapes bordered in silver metallic are appliqued. The lattice format expresses a "window-like" look at the ethereal world created by the transparent gauze, the light play on the jacquards and metallics and the flowing rivers of pieced silks.

AWARD FOR INNOVATIVE USE OF MATERIALS

Sharon Robinson. *Henry's Jacket.*
1983.
Pongee silk. Hand-dyed and hand-painted fabrics,
trapunto, quilted.

AWARD FOR ORIGINALITY OF DESIGN

Sharon Robinson. *Cathie's Jacket.*
1983.
Santa Rosa, California
Dupioni and pongee silk. Hand-dyed and hand-painted fabrics, trapunto, quilted.

AWARD FOR ORIGINALITY OF DESIGN

Loving the surface of a large piece of clean white silk, the artist can manipulate it using unseemly colors and push them as far as possible. She uses an abundance of texture and quit just before she has used too much. She can work her fabric into the form/silhouette of a costume that not only identifies it with a period of history, but also says, "Here I am, I am present."

Linda Levin. *The Space Between Two Mirrors.*
1984. 68" x 38"
Wayland, Ma.

Cottons, blends. Hand-dyed and hand-painted. Hand- and machine-pieced, hand-quilted.

The stimulus for this quilt came from the tree-like forms the artist created with fabric paint in mono-print technique. They suggested the stark shapes revealed when winter strips the foliage from trees and shrubs, and the patterns of light and shadow become strong and clear.

AWARD FOR ORIGINALITY OF CONCEPT

30

Linda Levin. *Description Without Place.*
1984. 53" x 47"
Wayland, Ma.
Cottons, blends. Hand- and machine-pieced.

A painter friend keeps the artist supplied with her used paint rags and paint-stained shirts. Used with her own dyed and painted fabrics they created a menacing, stormy atmosphere in which she floated island-like forms.

AWARD FOR ORIGINALITY OF CONCEPT

Virginia Jacobs. *Cunninghams' Constellations.*
1981. 108" x 54"
Philadelphia, Pa.
Cottons, blends, metallic lamé, beads. Applique, piecing and quilting.

The interior section was based on an embroidered Japanese theatre banner that the artist saw at an antique fair. She had originally planned to surround it with a quilted border resembling the brocades used to back Japanese scrolls depicting a giant chrysanthemum, and she attended a concert of Scottish folk music by the Silly Wizard Band and was so inspired by the vitality, humor and music of band members, that she decided to create a tartan border instead.

INVITATIONAL.

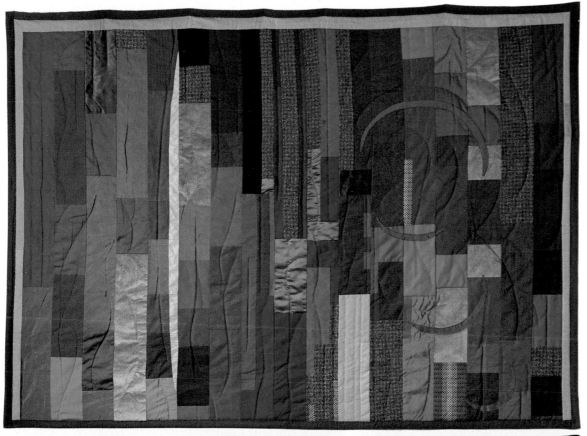

Susan Hoffman. *Soundings (Diptych).*
1979. 83½" x 123"
Livingston, New York
Machine-pieced, hand-appliqued, hand-quilted.

Barbara Packer. *Ruy Lopez.*
1984. 72" x 72"
New York, New York
Cottons, blends, Viyella, satin. Machine-pieced, hand-quilted.

INVITATIONAL

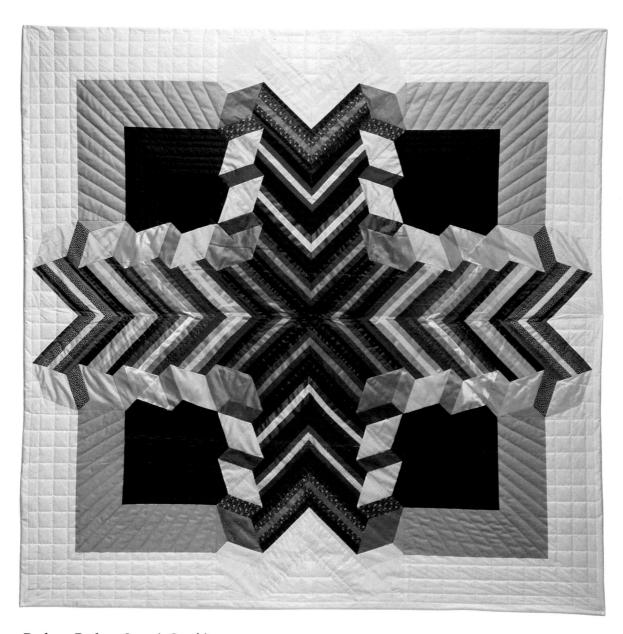

Barbara Packer. *Queen's Gambit.*
1984. 72" x 72"
New York, New York
Cottons, blends, Viyella, satin. Machine-pieced, hand-quilted.

Queen's Gambit and Ruy Lopez are two well known chess openings. While playing the game the artist became fascinated with the two-dimensionality or "flatness" of the chess board. These works are two efforts at exploring this characteristic common to paintings and quilts. While the maquettes appeared "flat," the actual quilts show unexpected spacial illusion!

INVITATIONAL

Elizabeth A. Busch.
Haystack Sunrise.
1984. 60" x 41"
Bangor, Maine
Cotton canvas, cotton, procion dyes,
oil crayons, polyblends, pillow tick-
ing. Machine-and hand-pieced,
machine-and hand-quilted, hand-
appliqued.

The Maine environment and architecture influence this work. The
artist lets the fabric dictate what she
does, whether it's hand-painted or
purchased. She never has a
preconceived notion of her work; it
happens as she's pinning pieces to her
studio wall.

Liz Alpert.
Good Morning Honey,
Sit Down.
1984. 23¾" x 19½"
Brighton, Ma.
Cotton and silk.
Applique and reverse
applique.

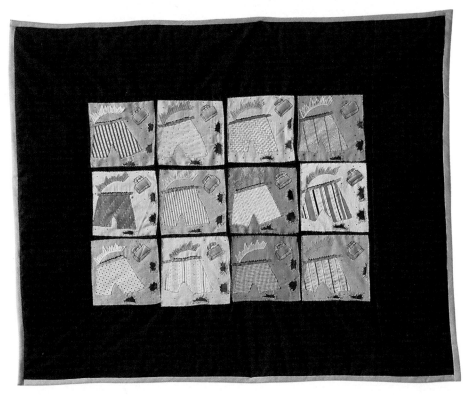

Nancy Crow. *Passion I.*
1984. 72" x 72"
Baltimore, Ohio
Cottons and cotton blends. Strip-piecing and piecing.
Quilted by the Amish

The artist's most intense interest lies in the exploration of unusual color relationships based on a combination of emotional/intellectual attitudes influenced by the tension of living in solitude (on a farm) while at times intensely craving human stimulation. She is particularly interested in the ideas of COURAGE, RESILIENCE, SELF-DISCIPLINE, DRIVE, INTENSITY, PASSION, COMPASSION, and the PRODUCTION OF A BODY OF WORK despite great obstacles, be they physical or mental or both.

INVITATIONAL

Carolyn A. Tolliver. *Untitled Triangles V.*
1984. 63" x 63"
Olivet, Michigan
Cotton, blends. Machine-pieced, hand-quilted.
Quilted by Mrs. Leroy Kline.

"Constructing" a geometric quilt such as this one is particularly interesting to the artist because she is attracted to the use of analogous colors to achieve an overall pleasing result, yet to retain a visual impact that lingers in the viewer's mind. She finds her quilt restful yet fresh and crisp.

Carolyn A. Tolliver. *Fractured Octagon I.*
1984. 52" x 52"
Olivet, Michigan
Cotton, blends. Machine-pieced and hand-quilted
Quilted by Mrs. Leroy Kline.

This quilt was constructed for the purpose of ordering the analogous rusts and blues within the neutral grid. The piece is pleasant yet vibrant and captures the eye, making it "twinkle." The curved corner shape arose from the need to balance the color against gray, tempering the metallic steel feeling into a softer overall one.

Carole Zarlin. *Helaine's Jacket.*
1981.
Roslyn, New York
Satin and silk. Cathedral window, hand-pieced.
This jacket was commissioned to be worn at Maxim's in Paris on New Year's Eve. The timing was most fortuitous, as the style of men's neckties was changing from wide to narrow, providing the silk inserts.

INVITATIONAL

Sonya Lee Barrington. *Checking It Out!*
1984. 44" x 44"
San Francisco, California
Cotton, blends. Machine-pieced and hand-quilted.

"Checking it Out!" was the next logical step in the artist's Curved Seam Series. She first worked using asymmetrical blocks, then gradually moved into using different kinds of symmetry. This piece presented a special problem. What to do with design around the axis when you want to make a 9-patch using bi-lateral symmetry and an underlying over-all pattern of checkerboards. You see the solution.

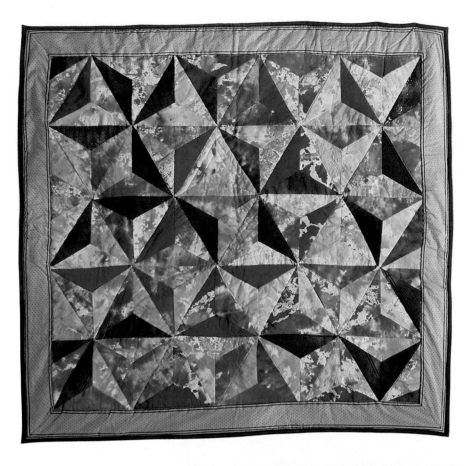

Sally Snow-Ekland.
Twilit Stars.
1984. 35" x 35"
Assonet, Mass.
Cotton. Hand-dyed,
machine-pieced, hand-
quilted.

This quilt is made from
one shape, so it is really
an exercise in color. The
overlapping stars reflect
the warmth of the setting
sun.

Barbara L. Crane.
Animal Magnetism.
1983. 40" x 40"
Lexington, Mass.
Cottons, blends, ivory
and glass. Machine-
pieced, hand-appliqued,
hand-quilted.

The artist was thinking
here of the wonder of
animal form — its diver-
sity and beauty. The tiny
white animals might be
seen as seeds: hardly
distinguished from each
other at any distance,
they nevertheless materi-
alize (pun intended!) into
wonderfully articulated
and specialized species.
And then they meet their
mates and the miracu-
lous process begins
again...

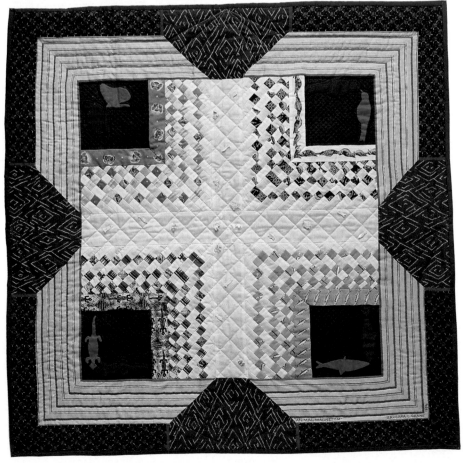

L. Carlene Raper. *Shades Afloat.*
1984. 94" x 74"
Cotton. Machine-pieced, tied.

After deciding on the simple
geometry of the pattern and cutting
the pieces from all the scraps
available, the artist pinned the
pieces to a board, stepping back to
see the color effects. She worked on
one quarter of the piece at a time,
sewing each quadrant together as it
was ready.

L. Carlene Raper. *Night Swallows.*
1983. 95" x 83"
Putney, Vermont
Cotton, Machine-pieced,
hand-quilted

Pat Gaska. *Boxed In.*
1983. 45½" x 69½"
Rothschild, Wisconsin
Cottons, blends. Machine-pieced, hand-appliqued, hand-quilted.

Most of the artist's work at this time deals with the concept of using light, medium and dark fabrics within basic geometric shapes to make a flat surface appear three-dimensional. This piece reflects, both in color and title, a particular mood — it was designed at a time when she felt "Boxed In." She especially likes this piece because it is true to the tradition of early patchwork quilts.

Sue H. Rodgers. *Fusion.*
1984. 62" x 62"
Mt. Lakes, N.J.
Cotton. Hand-quilted, trapunto.

The design elements of the panels are emphasized by the use of trapunto, and were created by overlapping and interlocking squares. Starting with the white panel and working clockwise, each panel becomes more complex, culminating in the black version which "fuses" the interlocking squares with heavy background quilting.

INVITATIONAL

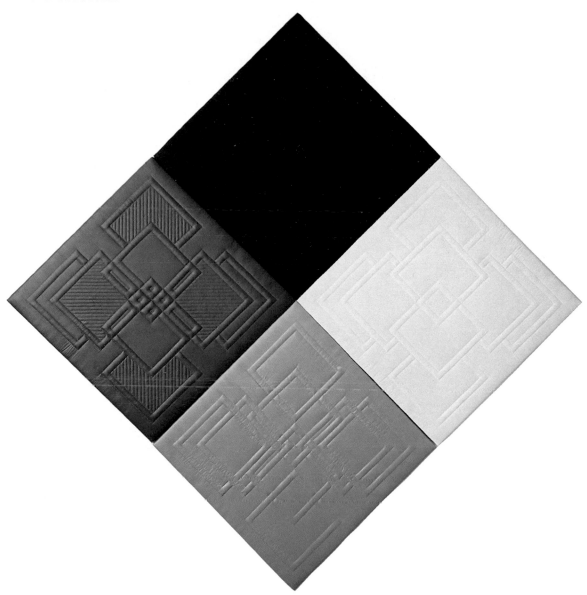

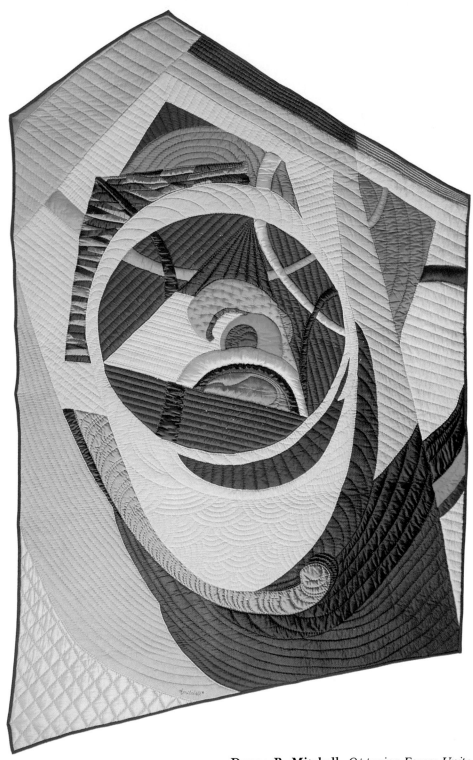

Donna B. Mitchell. *Opposing Forces Unite,*
also known as *The Battle of the Sexes Resolved.*
1982. 96" x 66"
Santa Cruz, Ca.
Silk. Pieced and appliqued and quilted.

Driven by the urge to create with her hands and directed by a love of beauty and color, the artist strives to create that which has not been seen before, art that is beautiful, to be savored, a positive force to combat the negative. She seeks the power to evoke beauty, an elusive and compelling search which sustains her spiritually and emotionally.
She works specifically with fabric because the techniques are most familiar, and because the fabrics themselves are much more inspiring and exciting materials than a cold lump of clay or a tube of paint.

Françoise Barnes. *Scorpio 3.*
1984. 80" x 80"
Athens, Ohio
Cottons, blends. Machine-pieced and applique, hand-quilted.
Quilted by Mrs. Leroy Kline

This quilt is the third of a triptych entitled SCORPIO; inspired by insects, both ferocious and ferocious-looking, by the mystery and enigma of painted faces and masks, and by the ceremonial costumes of Papua New Guinea tribesmen, this work is not intended for the shy, the meek or the gentle soul enamored of heart collections, victorian elegance and laces. It is intended to quicken the viewer's pulse for it talks about pain, joy, torment, ecstasy and laughter. It talks about LIFE, not mere existence; it demands from the viewer to participate and to be willing to take risks...

INVITATIONAL

Karen Gallogly. *Fields VI.*
1983. 53" x 53"
Villanova, Pa.
Blends. Machine-pieced
and hand-quilted.

In the Fields quilts intricately colored triangles work against one another so that they alternately flow into and limit one another.

Bobbie Fuhrmann.
Stepping Stones with Storm at Sea Border.
1983. 91" x 84"
Lancaster, New York
Cottons. Hand-pieced, hand-quilted.

The artist has always loved traditional patterns and tries to incorporate them into her quilts in innovative and untraditional ways. This quilt is a variation on the "Stepping Stones" pattern and has "Storm at Sea," traditionally an allover design used as a border motif. It is approximately 7,500 pieces.

Ann Bird. *Capital Star.*
1984. 71" x 71"
Ottawa, Canada
Cottons. Machine-pieced, hand-quilted.

This is a tribute to the Eternal Flame which glows constantly on the hill in front of Canada's Parliament Buildings in the Capital city of Ottawa. A mandala is a schematized representation of the cosmos, chiefly characterized by a concentric organization of geometric shapes. The centre is the beginning of the mandala. In the centre lies eternity.

Janice Ohlson Richards. *Tribute to Tippi Hedren.*
1984. 64" x 54"
Fox Island, Washington
Cottons, corduroy, velveteen, satin. Machine-pieced, hand-quilted.

The idea originated from a 10" module design, which is repeated throughout the quilt, by being set in different positions. Once the idea of the "bird" developed, the artist decided to carry through the idea of the birds flying from sunrise down into the sunset, and out into darkness. Thus it was named: "Tribute to Tippi Hedren."

Materials other than plain cottons were used to give it more depth and texture. Small pieces of satin were strip-pieced with the background cottons, to help show the reflection of the sun.

Mary Butler Shannon. *Starlight Unbounded.*
1984. 64" x 56"
Bergenfield, New Jersey
Cotton, blends, silk, antique satin. Machine-pieced, hand-quilted, embroidered.

After seeing the Picasso retrospective the artist was inspired by the colors and rhythms in the painting "The Milliner's Workshop." She originally envisioned this as a gigantic snowflake against a gray sky. However, the movement in the cubic projectiles haunted her and she felt compelled to incorporate the material into the piece. The red/green clashed with the gray and white; a metaphorsis ensued and suddenly the creation "exploded." She imagined this as the forces of nature in the heavens working during the birth of a new star.

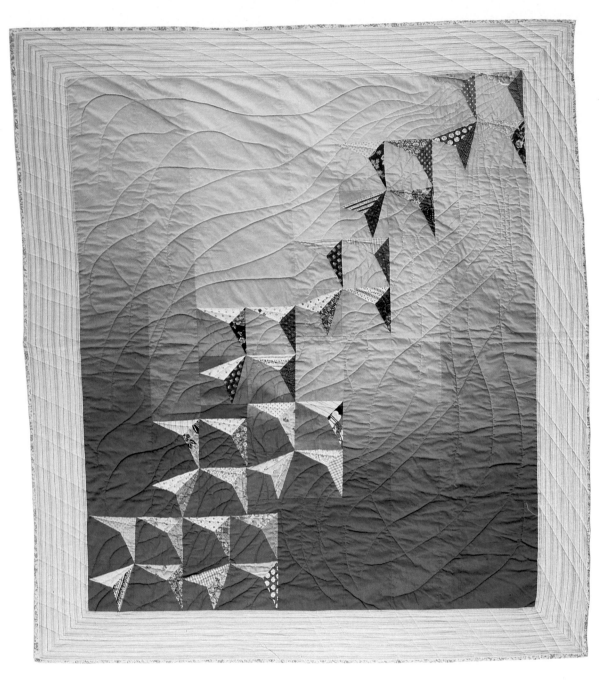

Nina Antze. *Bird Quilt.*
1983. 66" x 53"
Sebastopol, California
Cotton.

The artist has used the bird motif before in quilts. This bird quilt started as another triangle "scrap" quilt but evolved into a simpler design, as a needed contrast to its busier predecessors. The shaded background adds to the feeling of upward flight which was achieved with an easy bleaching technique.

EXCELLENCE OF WORKMANSHIP AWARD

Nina Antze. *Triangle Medallion.*
1983. 78" x 66"
Sebastopol, California
Cotton. Machine-pieced, hand-quilted.

This quilt was the first created by working directly with fabric. It was designed with triangles on a felt board.
The many different fabrics are reminiscent of the scrap bag quilts, in a more elegant and contemporary way.

EXCELLENCE OF WORKMANSHIP AWARD

Barbara L. Crane. *Foreign Exchange.*
1983. 52" x 52"
Lexington, Massachusetts
Cottons, coins. Machine-and hand-pieced, hand-quilted.

There was no thematic intent in this quilt. It was just fun with color and transparency effects, form (the take-off point was that plastic folding toy called "Flip-flops"), and quilting (with an attempt to make the lines heighten the sense of motion).

Jane Reeves. *Summer City.*
1983. 63" x 63"
Canton, Ohio
Cottons, blends. Machine-pieced, hand-quilted.
Quilted by Mrs. Aden Troyer

Working with strong color and large scale is something the artist enjoys, but when she finished this piece, its effect seemed as overpowering as the glare and heat of a work time traffic jam in July.

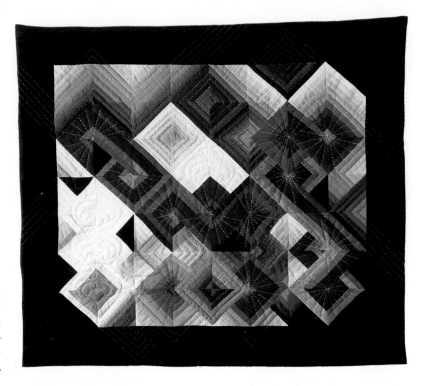

Paula Nadelstern. *Serendipity.*
1984. 30½" x 34"
Bronx, New York
Cottons, blends. Machine-
pieced, strip-piecing, hand-
quilted.

Serendipity is defined as an apparent aptitude for making fortunate discoveries accidentally, and is an apt description of this approach to quilt design. Intended as a graphic, this quilt was inspired as the artist's collection and interest in solid colors grew, after a long spell of designing appliqued pictorial block quilts. Through the physical action of placing the triangles, she discovered the ways to create visual movement. She took photographs of the quilt as it emerged, in an attempt to record its evolution.

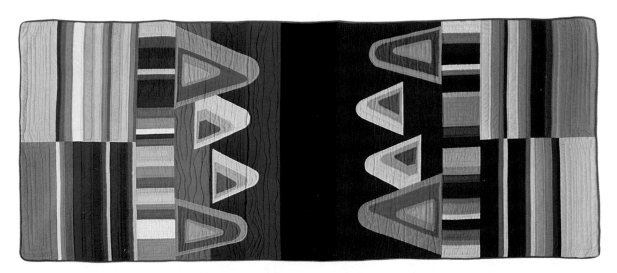

Lise Buonocore. *Morning, Evening.*
1983. 40" x 100"
River Falls, Wisconsin
Cotton. Pieced and appliqued.

In piecing her quilts together the artist deals with strong geometric shapes that frame or stand along side organic forms. These organic forms sometimes break away from the structure: thus adding a visual tension and a break with the symmetry, often associated with traditional quilts.

Joen Wolfrom.
Setting Sun.
1984. 36" x 46"
Fox Island, Wa.

This quilt was created to illustrate the method of representational strip piecing in textile art.

Dominie Nash. *Sea Fence.*
1983. 39½" x 40½"
Bethesda, Maryland
Cotton. Strip-pieced, machine-quilted, batik, dyed.

This was inspired by the juxtaposition of a wild landscape and a man-made dam during construction work on the Potomac River. The contrasts in color, form and material remained in the artist's memory until the specific design for the quilt evolved months later.

Pat Joyal. *Fredrique.*
1983. 54" x 66".
Duluth, Minnesota
Cotton, blends. Machine-pieced, strip-piecing.
Quilted by North Country Quilters

Brilliant colors and spatial illusions in quilts have always attracted the artist and she has intuitively gone in that direction in her own designs. She enjoys just looking at the bright fabrics on her shelves, thinking about possible combinations.

Pat Joyal. *Acanthus.*
1984. 60" x 48"
Duluth, Minnesota
Cotton, blends. Machine-pieced, strip-piecing, hand-quilted.
Quilted by J & C Stitchery

The blocks for Acanthus were very simple units that could be assembled in a variety of ways. The final choice created what was the greatest illusion of depth.

Donna M. Stader.
Etude VI: Golden Grid.
1984. 71" x 64"
Indianapolis, Indiana
Cottons, blends. Machine-pieced
and hand-quilted.

The Etude series of quilts marked the beginning of the quiltmaker's sense of herself as a quilt artist. It allowed her to express her individual color sense and to explore the inherent possibilities of a single pattern. It generated a desire to share these expressions with others. The work itself is the best record of the process and reasons behind its existence, even if they are not immediately evident.

Virginia P. Lefferdink.
(Knot)².
1984. 45¾" x 45¾" x 1½"
New York, N.Y.
Cotton, blends. Machine-pieced, trapunto, hand-quilted.

In retrospect this wall quilt appears to be an ontogenic reference to an insulated environment of small spaces in a teeming, ever-in-motion city, surrounded by seemingly random factors from which order occasionally emerges. While, the title, (Knot)², suggested itself from the central stuffed shapes, the artist prefers to consider it a pun on the problems of construction.

Georgia Springer. *Rhythmic Repeat.*
1984. 40" x 40"
Raleigh, N.C.
Cotton. Machine-pieced, machine-quilted.

In the past year, the artist has concentrated on using color and color values in two ways. First she tried to make quilts with light effects where light shines, vibrates, emerges or radiates in various ways. Second, she worked to create the spatial illusion of depth on the flat surface. Using the yellow light was her primary interest. By using the dynamic yellow concentric design, she wanted the viewer to be drawn into the quilt immediately and then, intrigued, to look longer, discovering the more subtle richness of the background fabrics.

Ruth B. McDowell. *Cherry People Pie.*
1984. 55" x 81".
Winchester, Mass.

Cottons, blends. Machine-pieced, hand-appliqued, hand-quilted.

This part of a series of wallhangings based on an extraordinary type of non-periodic tiling developed by the mathematician Roger Penrose. It is composed of two blocks — one kite-shaped and the other dart- or arrowhead-shaped. Some of the blocks are populated and others not.

INVITATIONAL

62

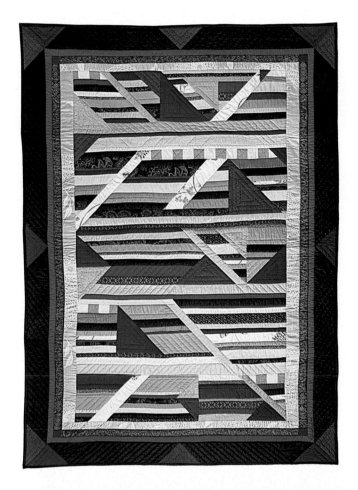

Paula Lederkramer. *Explorations.*
1983. 80" x 60"
Levittown, N.Y.
Cottons, blends. Hand-woven and hand-dyed fabrics. Hand- and machine-pieced, hand-quilted.

Explorations is an attempt to integrate many varied fabrics into one whole. It was not worked in blocks nor was it strip-pieced. The quilt developed intuitively. Quiltmaking has a long tradition of utilizing and recycling material and in her work the artist tries to continue this tradition, while developing new design ideas.

Susan Hoffman.
Constellation.
1982. 67" x 72½"
Livingston, New York
Machine-and hand-pieced, hand-quilted.

Esther Parkhurst. *July Study.*
1984. 41" x 60".
Los Angeles, Calif.
Cottons, blends. Machine- and strip-pieced, hand-quilted.
BEST IN SHOW

Jan Myers. *Zephyr.*
1984. 28" x 40"
Minneapolis, Minnesota
Cotton muslin. Machine strip-pieced, machine-quilted, hand-dyed.

The artist finds that working with dyed, pieced fabric not only frees her to work on almost any scale and have a product that is portable, it also involves a sensuous, hands-on medium that appeals to touch and answers the need for warmth. She is fascinated with color and light; she plays with space and change distances as gradations of color move in and out of the pieced surface. Most importantly, by working with pieced fabric, she can greatly extend the physical limits of her color fields.

INVITATIONAL

Linda Macdonald. *Clean Getaway.*
1983. 92" x 82"
Willits, California
Cotton. Machine-pieced, hand-appliqued, hand-quilted.

Juxtaposition of field to shape, pattern to void and object to nonobjective space interest the artist. The use of traditional quilting techniques for contemporary images creates a contrast contained in the piece. The quilt is two-sided, with the back being pieced simply, to better present the quilting without the reference of the front image.

Karen E. Dvorchak. *Scarlet Takes On Cool Red.*
1984. 54" x 54"
Littleton, Colorado
Cotton muslin. Machine-pieced and quilted, hand-dyed.

The artist is interested in the painterly effects of color in her quilts. Hand-dyeing each color gives her the same freedom as mixing paints on a palette. This quilt is a color study between shades of warm and cool red. After cutting out large and small squares of each gradation she played with the color arrangement on the floor until the design evolved. The smaller squares are fringed and fused to the larger squares, then the large squares are sewn into puff patches.

F. Bruce Wilcox. *Galxe Z.001.*

1984. 75" x 40".

Denver, Colo.

Cotton blends, acrylic Paint. Hand-quilted, padded.

Physical, mental, emotional, synthesis executed in fiber relief. Texture pattern finish motivated by all visual, aural, sensual, experiences in fantasy reality — past, present, future, producing being.

68

Suzanne Stout. *Murder of Crows.*
1983. 38" x 30"
Milwaukee, Wisconsin
Microfiche, computer tape, roll-leaf stamping tape, various film, and Mylar. Machine-pieced.

The artist's work is highly reflective of our own creation of technology. Traditionally, the quilt symbolizes warmth and comfort with patterns handed down from generations past. Microfiche, movie film, and computer tape seem highly impersonal and yet, one small space of tape or film may hold an individual's entire identity. Assembling these materials into a quilt form is a break in tradition. Technology is all around us, from the plastic bag a sandwich is wrapped in, to the synthetics in your clothing, to video games and to a home computer.

Diane Ruble. *Dissolution.*

1984. 40" x 52"

Kent, Ohio

Cotton, blends. Machine-strip-pieced, hand-quilted.

This work was created in the heart of an austere winter. It was worked more intuitively than earlier work. Bright or glowing areas emerge from the subdued boundaries and quite appropriately reflect the artist's innermost feeling that there is positive in every negative. There can be great opportunity for personal, even artistic, growth in adverse conditions.

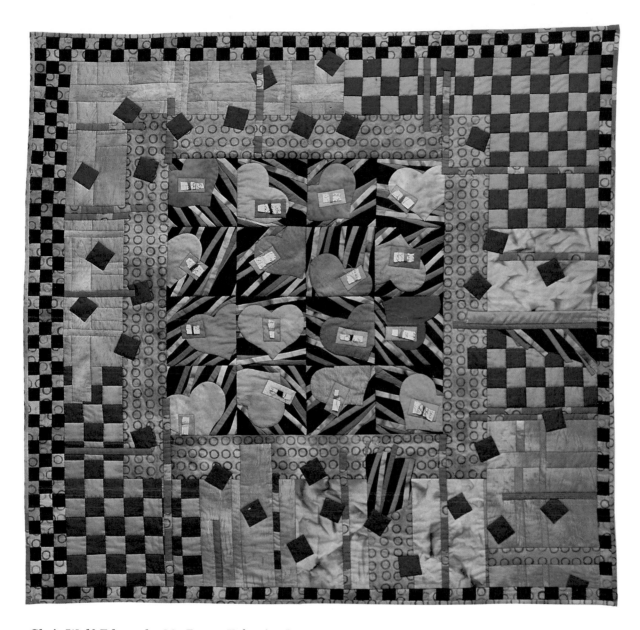

Chris Wolf Edmonds. *My Funny Valentine I.*
1984. 44" x 43"
Lawrence, Kansas
Cotton, thread-wrapped torn paper. Hand-appliqued, machine-pieced and quilted, hand-painted.

The artist finds she is continuously influenced by friends and their work. In the "Valentine" series she let some of this influence show through her spontaneous approach to the construction. The influence exerts itself sometimes through color impressions, form, or even materials received through personal friendships with specific individuals.

INVITATIONAL

Jane Reeves. *HURRY UP PLEASE ITS TIME.*
1983 72" x 72"
Canton, Ohio
Cottons, blends, Machine-pieced, hand-quilted.
Quilted by Mrs. Elmer Kemph

The title comes from T.S. Eliot's "The Wasteland." In designing the piece the artist wanted to present a strong contrast between the dark and light areas and to create the illusion that it was illuminated from behind.

Jane Reeves. *Arcadia.*
1983. 63" x 63"
Canton, Ohio
Cottons, blends. Machine-pieced, hand-quilted.
Quilted by Emma Hershberger

Blocks of the same design in three sizes were used to construct this quilt. The increasing scale presents different views and changes the effect and emphasis of the design. The colors were chosen to evoke the spirit of Renaissance pastoral poetry.

Linda Levin. *A Clear Day and No Memories.*
1984. 62" x 44"
Wayland, Ma.
Cotton, blends. Hand-and machine-pieced.

The intent was to show the idealized, non-specific city set against a wind-swept sky and reduced to pattern, color and shape.

AWARD FOR ORIGINALITY OF CONCEPT

Sherry Miller. *American Landscape Quilt.*
1984. 72" x 62"
Portland, Maine
Acrylic and canvas. 42 individual paintings machine-stitched.

Jean Crist. *Round-tu-it.*
1982. 39" x 39"
Rockville Centre, N.Y.
Cotton. Machine-pieced, hand-quilted.

Only another quilter knows how many projects she can have going on at one time. By the time the artist got around to finishing this one — it had a fitting name — "Round-tu-it!" She found this design exciting to work on because of its constant motion. Even the quilting was fun as it followed the fluid design right out to its borders.

INVITATIONAL

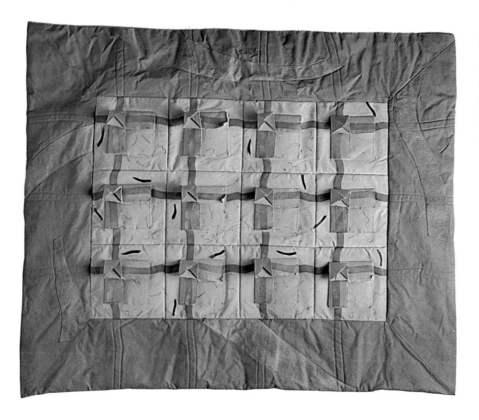

Susan Ferrari Rowley.
The Common Thread.
1984. 48" x 56" x2½"
Churchville, New York
Cotton, handmade
paper, stainless steel.
Pieced, folded, quilted,
painted, dyed.

Being very interested in
the changes that must
take place in technique
and materials, to trans-
form from a two dimen-
sional surface to one of
relief, the artist takes
visual cues from tradi-
tional quilts and trans-
lates them into personal
statements, making full
utilization of contem-
porary opportunities.

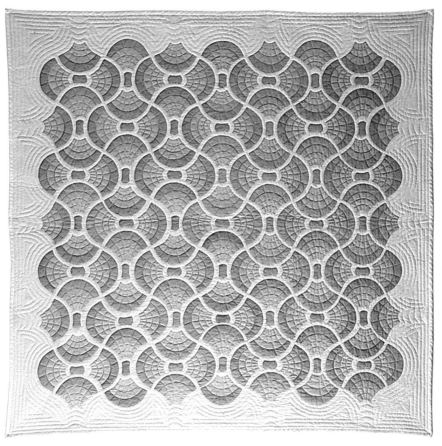

Hallie H. O'Kelly.
Mollusca.
1984. 40" x 40"
Tuscaloosa, Alabama
Cotton. Silk-screened
and hand-quilted.

The ocean was the
inspiration for this quilt.
The oscillating white
lines symbolize wave
action and the design
within these lines suggests
sea shells. The colors
were chosen because they
are common to many
shells.

Loretta Krieger. *Star.*
1984. 42" x 90"
Massapequa Park, New York
Cotton, blends. Hand-pieced, hand-quilted.

INVITATIONAL

JURORS' STATEMENTS

Jan Myers

A statement that bears repeating is that a juried show reflects the biases and pleasures of the jurors. Selection for this show was difficult. With few exceptions the work was well thought out and skillfully executed. The greatest difficulty in jurying this show was the necessity to eliminate some outstanding work because it was determined not to meet our definition of "original" or "original adaptation of traditional." In several cases it was necessary to make a choice between workmanship and originality. Compromises were made to stay within the definition of the show, striving at the same time to select a show that would best reflect the diversity and quality of entries received.

One strong trend evident in this group of entries, was toward altering materials. Efforts to make quilts that are Art seem in many instances to be quilts that move in some physical way into the realms of painting or sculpture, the historically acceptable "art forms." Fabrics were dyed, painted, imprinted with photo images before piecing. While these techniques are not new in 1985, their prevalence seemed significant. Several entries employed non-fabric materials: mylar, metal, paper, plastic. Although I have no objection to classifying these pieces as quilts, I personally feel that novelty of materials is not enough to override mediocre design. It seems clear that as quilts are gaining recognition as art, various non-traditional techniques are being explored, stretching the boundaries of "quilt-ness." Hopefully the makers will not lose sight of the precision construction, the sculpted quilting, the soul and the sensuousness that historically defines "quilt." It was my challenge in jurying this show to reflect these trends, while keeping design and workmanship as primary determinates for acceptance.

Chris Wolf Edmonds

When I was invited to jury the Nassau County Quilt Expo '85 show, I was delighted. It sounded like great fun to sit and look at slides of quilts for two days (and it was), but the task of selecting a limited number of quilts from scores of hopeful entrants is an awesome responsibility. It is a responsibility not only to the individuals who have put themselves and their work on the line, but to the state of the art as a whole. The pieces selected for such a show demonstrate the direction of contemporary quiltmaking today.

While the selection process is necessarily subjective, it is perhaps less so as the result of using a panel of jurors rather than a single judge. Although our individual preferences were at some times apparent, and probably provided for a more balanced show, I felt that the three of us as jurors generally agreed about what we were looking for in quality of design and workmanship. More important we seemed to agree on a more intuitive level when we saw the few pieces that were truly new and original work. This made it easy to select those pieces which were to receive the top awards for the show from among those accepted. I would rather have had a more difficult task.

While there were a great many quilts which appeared to exhibit high quality workmanship and appealing color and design, I would like to have seem more quilts which also excited me. I would like to have seen more that thrilled and intrigued my senses...more new...more original...more growth and change in the quiltmaker's art. As a juror, a teacher, an artist, I encourage today's quiltmakers to treasure and admire the great heritage of traditional quilt patterns and techniques, but to be more than emulators. Don't be satisfied with excellent repetitions. Take the art a step further. Add to the heritage.

Françoise Barnes

Jurying a national quilt show is a mixed blessing for me: I know I will be able to look at the broad spectrum of quiltmaking across the country and this is always a joy, since quiltmaking is what I do and what I love.

I assume that I will see new ideas, rich and exciting colors, quilts so different from my own work that I will go home invigorated, enriched, stimulated. I also know that I will have to contemplate quite a few tepid, unchallenging warmed-up oldies!

This was the case for Quilt Expo '85. There was excitement and there were the usual "cutesies". Yet it was a great pleasure working with Chris and Jan and a great satisfaction, after many long hours, to select a show which is, indeed a very good one, with some truly wonderful pieces.

It is time for quiltmakers who desire to commit themselves to this art form to seek new inspirations, perhaps to turn more energetically towards the Fine Arts, as, in my opinion, the richest, most meaningful source of inspiration and stimulation.

We have the talent; we have the heart; we need integrity, we need a vision. Now is the time to *not* think pretty, to *not* think safe but to think Art first. *Art,* that is what this is all about, that *is* the challenge.

INDEX